- ✦ **History**
- ✦ **Evidence**
- ✦ **Tools**
- ✦ **Techniques**
- ✦ **Myths**
- ✦ **+ more**

The quick guide to the NINJA

Secrets of the shinobi revealed

DISCLAIMER

Please note we are **NOT RESPONSIBLE** in any manner whatsoever for any injury that may result from practicing the techniques and / or instructions given within. Since the physical activities described herein may be too strenuous in nature for some readers to engage in safely, it is essential that medical advice is sought prior to any training.

First edition
INSIDE NINJUTSU
England

忍 CONTENTS

Introduction   7

FIRE SCROLL | Background   9

WATER SCROLL | Methods   26

WIND SCROLL | Equipment   49

EARTH SCROLL | Legacy   60

The quick guide to the
NINJA
Secrets of the shinobi revealed

忍 INTRODUCTION

The ninja and the samurai were distinct groups of people in feudal Japan, with different skills, training, and social status. While some ninja may have been samurai, and some samurai may have trained in ninja skills, the two groups were not always synonymous.

The samurai were members of the warrior class in feudal Japan and were highly skilled in combat and swordsmanship. They were loyal to a lord or daimyo and served as their retainers, protecting their lands and serving in their armies. The samurai followed a strict code of honor known as bushido and were highly respected in Japanese society.

The ninja, on the other hand, were covert agents who specialized in espionage, sabotage, and on rare ocassions assassination. They operated outside of the samurai class and often worked as mercenaries or freelancers. The ninja were highly skilled in disguise, infiltration, and unconventional warfare, and were often used by samurai lords as spies or assassins.

While there may have been some overlap between the two groups, the ninja were generally viewed as outside of the traditional social hierarchy of feudal Japan. They were often seen as outsiders or even outcasts, and their methods were sometimes viewed as dishonorable by the samurai.

In any case, their methods and skills have been the subject of fascination and intrigue for centuries, and have given rise to many myths and legends. However, the true history of the ninja is shrouded in mystery and ambiguity, making it difficult to separate fact from fiction.

This book is an exploration of the history, methods, myths, and legacy of the ninja. It will examine the historical context in which the ninja emerged, the various techniques and tools they used, and the role they played in Japanese society.

Additionally, it will explore the myths and legends surrounding the ninja, and how they have been portrayed in popular culture.

The book is divided into several sections, each covering a different aspect of the ninja. Overall, it will provide a rounded overview of these ancient spies, examining both their historical reality and their cultural significance. It is intended for anyone fascinated by the legendary figures who have captured our imaginations for centuries.

火

THE
FIRE SCROLL
SECTION ONE

The ninja in context

SHINOBI

A shinobi is a term used to refer to a member of the ninja, a group of covert agents and mercenaries who operated in feudal Japan. The term "shinobi" is often used interchangeably with "ninja," although some scholars suggest that the two terms may have slightly different meanings.

Shinobi were known for their skills in infiltration, espionage, and supposedly assassination, as well as their ability to operate in secrecy and avoid detection. They were often hired by feudal lords or other powerful figures to carry out covert operations, gather intelligence, or eliminate rivals or enemies.

The kanji for "ninja" (忍者) is composed of two parts:

"Nin" (忍) which means "to endure" or "to conceal." It consists of two smaller components: "ren" (刃) which means "blade" or "edge," and "kokoro" (心) which means "heart" or "mind." Together, these components suggest the idea of "enduring the blade" or "concealing the heart/mind."

"Ja" (者) which means "person" or "individual." This component is commonly used in Japanese to indicate a particular profession or role, such as "sensei" (teacher) or "kaisha-sha" (company employee).

Together, the two components suggest the idea of a person who is skilled in the art of endurance and concealment, which reflects the core abilities of a ninja.

NINJUTSU

Ninjutsu is a collection of skills, techniques, and strategies associated with the ninja, a group of covert agents and mercenaries who operated in feudal Japan. While the term "ninjutsu" literally means "the art of the ninja," it encompasses a wide range of skills beyond just combat and assassination.

Ninjutsu includes skills like stealth, disguise, espionage, sabotage, and infiltration, as well as techniques with various tools and weapons like shuriken and the katana. In addition to physical skills, ninjutsu also encompasses mental and spiritual disciplines like meditation, visualization, and the cultivation of an unbreakable will.

While much of the historical information about the ninja and their practices has been lost over time, modern practitioners of ninjutsu seek to preserve and continue the legacy of these skilled and resourceful agents.

Some schools of ninjutsu focus primarily on the physical techniques of combat and infiltration, while others place a greater emphasis on the spiritual and philosophical aspects of the art.

Overall, ninjutsu is a complex and multifaceted art that encompasses a wide range of skills and practices.

ORIGINS

The origins of the ninja, also known as shinobi, are not well-documented, and much of what is known about them is shrouded in mystery and legend. The ninja were a group of warriors and spies who emerged in feudal Japan during the 15th century.

It is believed that the ninja developed as a response to the political instability and warfare that plagued Japan during this period. They were initially hired as mercenaries and scouts by warring factions, but eventually developed their own unique set of skills and techniques that set them apart from other warriors.

The ninja were known for their stealth, espionage, and sabotage tactics, which allowed them to gather intelligence, infiltrate enemy territories, and carry out covert missions without being detected. They also adopted a wide range of specialized weapons and tools, such as shuriken (throwing stars), kusarigama (sickle and chain), and smoke bombs. Although they had few to call their own.

The exact origins of the ninja are debated, and there are several theories about where they came from. Some historians believe that they were descended from the yamabushi, a group of mountain hermits who practiced a form of esoteric Buddhism and were known for their martial skills. Others speculate that they were influenced by Chinese secret societies or that they evolved from the samurai class.

Despite their mysterious origins, the ninja have become a popular icon in popular culture, and their legacy continues to fascinate and inspire people around the world.

DEVELOPMENT

The ninja evolved over time to adapt to changing political and social circumstances in Japan. Their techniques, tactics, and equipment changed in response to new challenges and opportunities.

During the 15th and 16th centuries, the ninja were primarily employed as mercenaries and spies by warring factions in Japan. They were trained in infiltration, sabotage, and assassination techniques, and were often used to gather intelligence about enemy movements and fortifications.

As the ninja's reputation grew, they began to develop a more independent role in Japanese society.

Some ninja clans established themselves as powerful independent forces, and were able to influence politics and warfare on a larger scale.

In the 17th and 18th centuries, the ninja became associated with the martial arts schools that emerged in Japan. They were trained in a variety of weapons and techniques, and became known for their skills in swordsmanship, archery, and hand-to-hand combat.

During the Edo period (1603-1868), the ninja's role in Japanese society changed once again. With the consolidation of power under the Tokugawa shogunate, the ninja were no longer needed for espionage and warfare, and many turned to other occupations. Some became farmers or artisans, while others continued to practice their martial arts and passed down their techniques to future generations.

Today, the ninja's legacy lives on in popular culture, and their techniques and weapons continue to be studied and practiced by martial arts enthusiasts around the world. While their exact origins and history remain shrouded in mystery, the ninja's impact on Japanese history and culture cannot be denied.

EVIDENCE

Yes, there is evidence that the ninja, or shinobi, really existed in feudal Japan. While much of what is known about the ninja comes from folklore, legends, and popular culture, there are historical documents and artifacts that support their existence.

For example, there are several historical texts from the 16th and 17th centuries that mention the ninja, including the "Bansenshukai" and the "Shoninki." These texts describe the ninja's techniques, equipment, and tactics, and provide detailed instructions on how to become a ninja.

In addition, there are several historical accounts of the ninja carrying out covert missions and acts of sabotage during wartime. For example, in the 16th century, the ninja were used by warlords to infiltrate and sabotage enemy fortifications, and were often successful in their missions.

While much of the ninja's history and legacy remains shrouded in mystery and legend, there is enough historical evidence to suggest that they were a real group of warriors and spies who played an important role in Japanese history and culture.

SCROLLS

The "Bansenshukai" is a historical text from 17th century Japan that provides information about ninja techniques and tactics. The title "Bansenshukai" translates to "All-Encompassing Book on the Art of Ninjutsu."

The author of the "Bansenshukai" is Fujibayashi Saburo, a member of a ninja clan in Iga Province. The book is divided into 22 volumes and contains detailed information about the skills and techniques used by the ninja. This includes information on disguise, espionage, infiltration, assassination, and other covert operations.

The "Bansenshukai" is considered one of the most important texts on ninjutsu, and is often used as a reference by martial arts practitioners and historians interested in the history of the ninja. It provides valuable insight into the training and tactics used by the ninja during the feudal period in Japan.

The "Shoninki" is a 17th-century Japanese text that provides a detailed description of the techniques, strategies, and tactics used by the ninja. The title "Shoninki" translates to "True Path of the Ninja's House."

The author of the "Shoninki" is Natori Masatake, a samurai from the province of Kii who was also a skilled practitioner of ninjutsu.

The book is based on his extensive knowledge and experience of the ninja tradition, and provides an inside look at the secret world of the ninja.

The "Shoninki" is considered one of the most important texts on ninjutsu, as it provides valuable information on the mindset, skills, and techniques used by the ninja during the feudal period in Japan. The book covers a wide range of topics, including disguise, espionage, infiltration, assassination, and other covert operations. It also provides insights into the philosophical and spiritual aspects of the ninja tradition.

The "Shoninki" is still widely read and studied by martial artists and historians interested in the history of the ninja, and it remains an important resource for anyone interested in the history and techniques of ninjutsu.

SHONINKI CONTENTS

The "Shoninki" is a detailed text that covers a wide range of topics related to the practice of ninjutsu. The book is divided into four main sections:

1. The first section covers the history and philosophy of ninjutsu, as well as the essential skills and attitudes required for success as a ninja. This section includes discussions on the importance of secrecy, deception, and self-discipline, as well as the basic techniques and tactics used by the ninja.
2. The second section focuses on the physical skills and techniques used by the ninja, including techniques for stealth, infiltration, disguise, and escape. This section also covers weapons and their use, including the use of throwing weapons, swords, and other weapons commonly used by the ninja.
3. The third section covers the art of assassination, including strategies for identifying and eliminating targets, as well as techniques for poisoning and other methods of killing.
4. The fourth and final section focuses on the spiritual and philosophical aspects of ninjutsu, including discussions on the nature of reality, the importance of self-discipline and self-awareness, and the role of meditation and other spiritual practices in the life of a ninja.

Overall, the "Shoninki" provides a comprehensive overview of the techniques, strategies, and attitudes required for success as a ninja, and is considered one of the most important texts on ninjutsu.

The Ninpiden is a historical text believed to have been written by Hattori Hanzo, a famous ninja who lived in the 16th century.

The Gunpo Jiyoshu is a military manual from the 16th century that includes sections on ninjutsu. It describes various techniques that could be used by the ninja. The manual also provides instructions on how to detect and defend against ninja attacks.

However, it is important to note that the Gunpo Jiyoshu is not solely dedicated to ninjutsu, and its description of ninja techniques is just one small part of the manual.

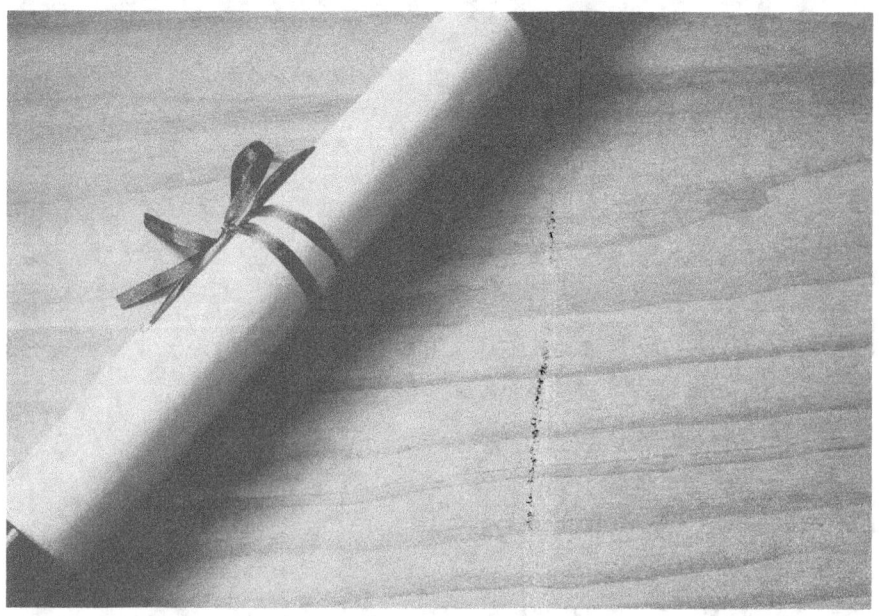

Additionally, while the manual does provide insight into some aspects of ninjutsu, it is not considered to be a comprehensive or authoritative source on the subject.

IGA NINJA

Iga Ryu ninjutsu is believed to have developed during the Sengoku period (1467-1615) in Japan. The region of Iga, located in present-day Mie Prefecture, was known for its mountainous terrain and dense forests, which made it a natural stronghold for guerrilla warfare and resistance against invading armies.

The Iga people were known for their resourcefulness, cunning, and ability to live off the land, and these skills were later incorporated into their ninjutsu techniques.

The men of Iga were known for their skills in ninjutsu. They lived in a mountainous region of Japan that was difficult to access and defend, which made it a prime target for attack. As a result, the people of Iga developed specialized skills in guerrilla warfare, espionage, and other forms of unconventional combat that came to be known as ninjutsu.

Additionally, the rugged terrain and isolation of the region allowed for the development of a unique culture and way of life that emphasized self-reliance, resilience, and adaptability, all qualities that were highly valued in the practice of ninjutsu.

SAMURAI VS NINJA

Oda Nobunaga, one of the most powerful daimyos (feudal lords) of the Sengoku period in Japan, had a complicated relationship with the ninja. On one hand, he recognized the usefulness of their skills in espionage and assassination, and employed many ninja in his service. On the other hand, he was also known to be distrustful of them and at times sought to eliminate them.

In the 1560s, Nobunaga was engaged in a power struggle with the Iga and Koka regions, which were known for their ninja clans. Despite his initial attempts to destroy these clans, Nobunaga eventually recognized their value and made peace with them. He even enlisted members of the Iga clan as his personal bodyguards and used ninja tactics in his battles.

However, in 1579, Nobunaga's relationship with the ninja soured once again when he suspected them of being involved in a plot to assassinate him. He ordered a massacre of the ninja in Iga, resulting in the deaths of an estimated 4,000 people. Despite this, some ninja continued to serve under Nobunaga and his successors, including Tokugawa Ieyasu.

HISTORICAL NINJA

There are many legendary and historical ninja figures, but one of the most famous is Hattori Hanzo (1541-1596), who was a samurai and the chief of the Iga ninja clan.

Hattori Hanzo was a skilled fighter and strategist, and was known for his loyalty to Tokugawa Ieyasu, who later became the shogun of Japan.

Hattori Hanzo played a pivotal role in several key battles and campaigns during the Warring States period of Japan, including the Battle of Sekigahara in 1600, which cemented the Tokugawa shogunate's control over Japan. He was also instrumental in helping Tokugawa Ieyasu escape from danger during a crucial battle in 1570.

Hattori Hanzo's reputation as a skilled fighter and leader has been passed down through history, and he has been featured in numerous movies, TV shows, and video games as a legendary ninja warrior. However, it is worth noting that some of the stories and legends associated with Hattori Hanzo may be based more on fiction than fact.

TOKUGAWA IEYASU ESCAPE

According to historical accounts, Hattori Hanzo played a crucial role in helping Tokugawa Ieyasu escape from danger during the Battle of Mikatagahara in 1572. During the battle, Ieyasu's forces were surrounded and outnumbered by the army of Takeda Katsuyori. In the midst of the chaos, Hattori Hanzo suggested that Ieyasu disguise himself as a servant and escape through the enemy lines.

Hattori Hanzo provided Ieyasu with a servant's outfit and arranged for him to be escorted out of the camp by a group of disguised soldiers. Hanzo himself stayed behind with a small group of loyal soldiers to hold off the enemy forces and create a diversion, allowing Ieyasu to escape safely.

Thanks to Hattori Hanzo's quick thinking and bravery, Ieyasu was able to avoid capture and went on to become one of the most powerful leaders in Japanese history. Hattori Hanzo's actions during the Battle of Mikatagahara earned him a reputation as a skilled strategist and leader, and he became a trusted ally of Ieyasu.

WWII NINJA

While there are no official records indicating that the Japanese military used ninjutsu during World War II, some historians speculate that certain aspects of ninjutsu, such as stealth and infiltration techniques, may have been incorporated into Japanese military training during the war. However, it's important to note that such claims remain largely speculative and lack concrete evidence.

The ninja have captured the popular imagination for centuries, and as a result, a number of myths and misconceptions have arisen about them.

NINJA MYTHS

Here are some common ninja myths:

1. Ninja wore all-black outfits: While it is true that the ninja often wore dark clothing to help them blend in with their surroundings, they did not exclusively wear all-black outfits. In fact, they often wore regular clothing or disguised themselves as ordinary civilians to avoid detection.
2. Ninja could walk on water: While some legends claim that the ninja had the ability to walk on water, this is a myth. It is more likely that they used special shoes or techniques to traverse shallow bodies of water, or simply avoided them altogether.
3. Ninja were all highly skilled martial artists: While the ninja were certainly skilled in hand-to-hand combat, not all of them were martial arts experts. Many were more focused on skills like disguise, espionage, and sabotage.
4. Ninja were all Japanese: While the ninja were primarily based in Japan, they were not exclusively Japanese. It is believed that some Korean and Chinese agents also trained in ninja skills and worked as mercenaries in Japan.
5. Ninja were always loyal to their employers: While the ninja were often hired by samurai lords to carry out missions, they were not always loyal to their employers. In fact, they were often hired by rival lords to carry out acts of espionage or sabotage against their original employer.

These are just a few examples of common myths about the ninja. While the truth about the ninja may never be fully known, separating fact from fiction can help us better understand their role in Japanese history and culture.

THE
WATER SCROLL
SECTION TWO

METHODS

NINJA TRAINING

The training methods of the ninja, also known as ninjutsu, were highly secretive and passed down through oral tradition and practical instruction from master to student. While the specific training methods varied depending on the particular school or style of ninjutsu, there were some common elements to ninja training.

One of the key components of ninja training was the development of mental focus and discipline. The ninja needed to be able to stay calm and focused under pressure, and to be able to make quick decisions in high-stress situations. To develop these skills, ninja trainees would often practice meditation, visualization, and other and other mental exercises.

The ninja also received training in espionage and infiltration techniques. This included learning how to gather intelligence, how to blend in with a crowd, how to disguise oneself, and how to pick locks.

Overall, the training methods of the ninja were highly varied and specialized, and involved a combination of physical conditioning, mental discipline, combat training, and espionage techniques.

NINJA FIGHTING ARTS

The ninja are associated with a variety of fighting techniques and martial arts, many of which have been passed down through generations of practitioners. However, it is important to note that the term "ninjutsu" refers to a collection of skills and practices associated with the ninja, rather than a specific martial art.

While some modern martial arts schools claim to teach "ninja fighting arts," it is difficult to say whether these techniques are truly representative of the historical practices of the ninja. This is because much of the information about the ninja has been lost over time, and what remains is often shrouded in legend and myth.

That being said, there are certainly martial arts techniques and practices that are associated with the ninja. These might include skills like stealth, disguise, and infiltration, as well as hand-to-hand combat techniques and the use of weapons like shuriken and the katana.

Ultimately, the true nature of ninja fighting arts is difficult to pin down, and much of what we know about the ninja and their skills is shrouded in mystery and legend. Nonetheless, the legacy of the ninja continues to inspire practitioners of martial arts and students of history and culture alike.

ART OF WAR

Sun Tzu's book "The Art of War" has had a significant influence on military strategy and tactics not only in China but also in Japan. While it is difficult to say exactly how much of an influence Sun Tzu had on Japan's ninja, it is likely that ninja were familiar with his teachings and may have incorporated some of his ideas into their own strategies and tactics.

Sun Tzu's book emphasizes the importance of deception, surprise, and intelligence gathering in warfare. These are all key elements of ninja tactics, so it is possible that ninja studied "The Art of War" and adapted its principles to their own methods.

For example, Sun Tzu emphasized the importance of understanding the terrain and adapting one's tactics accordingly.

Additionally, Sun Tzu emphasized the importance of avoiding direct confrontation whenever possible and instead focusing on using indirect methods to achieve one's objectives. This is similar to the ninja's use of sabotage, espionage, and assassination to achieve their goals.

While it is difficult to say exactly how much of an influence Sun Tzu had on Japan's ninja, it is likely that his ideas were familiar to them and may have influenced their tactics and strategies to some extent.

Sun Tzu's book "The Art of War" places great emphasis on the use of spies in warfare. He believes that intelligence gathering is essential to achieving victory, and that a successful commander must have a good understanding of the enemy's strengths, weaknesses, and intentions.

Sun Tzu says that spies should be used to gather information about the enemy's plans and movements, and to sow disinformation and confusion among the enemy ranks. He also advises that spies should be treated well and rewarded generously, as this will encourage them to continue to provide valuable information.

According to Sun Tzu, the best spies are those who are able to blend in with their surroundings and appear to be ordinary civilians or even members of the enemy's own army. They should be skilled at gathering information without being detected, and should be able to communicate this information quickly and effectively to their superiors.

Sun Tzu sees the use of spies as an essential tool for achieving victory in warfare, and his ideas have had a lasting impact on military strategy and tactics around the world.

In "The Art of War," Sun Tzu describes several different types of spies that can be used to gather information about the enemy. These include:

1. Local spies: These are people who are recruited from the local population and are familiar with the area and its inhabitants. They are often used to gather information about the enemy's movements and intentions.

2. Inward spies: These are individuals who are already working for the enemy and are recruited to provide information to the opposing side. They can be particularly valuable as they have access to sensitive information that might be difficult to obtain through other means.

3. Converted spies: These are individuals who are sent to infiltrate the enemy's camp and then defect to the other side. They are often used to sow disinformation and confusion among the enemy ranks.

4. Doomed spies: These are individuals who are sent on a mission with the expectation that they will be caught and interrogated by the enemy. They are given false information or partial information to feed to the enemy in order to mislead them.

Sun Tzu believed that the use of spies was an essential part of warfare, and that a successful commander must be skilled at recruiting and deploying spies effectively in order to gain an advantage over the enemy.

INTELLIGENCE GATHERING

Ninja were skilled at gathering all sorts of information, depending on the mission or objective they were given. Here are some examples of the types of information that ninja might gather:

1. Military intelligence: Ninja were often employed to gather information about enemy troop movements, fortifications, and battle plans. They would use a variety of methods, such as spying on enemy camps or intercepting messages, to gather this information.
2. Political intelligence: Ninja might be tasked with gathering information about political figures, such as their alliances, motives, and plans. This information could be used to gain an advantage in negotiations or to prevent political unrest.
3. Economic intelligence: Ninja might also gather information about economic activities, such as the production of valuable goods or the location of hidden resources. This information could be used to gain an economic advantage or to disrupt the enemy's economy.

4. Social intelligence: Ninja might gather information about the social dynamics of a particular area or group, such as the power structure, key individuals, or cultural norms. This information could be used to infiltrate a group or to manipulate social dynamics to the ninja's advantage.

5. Technological intelligence: Ninja might also gather information about new technologies or weapons being developed by the enemy. This information could be used to develop countermeasures or to gain a technological advantage.

INFILTRATION

Infiltrating a castle was one of the most difficult and dangerous missions that a shinobi could undertake. However, there were several techniques and strategies that they used to increase their chances of success.

One common approach was to disguise themselves as ordinary travelers or merchants and enter the castle through its main gate. Shinobi would often carry forged documents or other forms of identification to help them blend in and avoid suspicion. Once inside the castle, they would use their skills in disguise and deception to move around unnoticed and gather intelligence on the castle's defenses, layout, and key personnel.

Another approach was to infiltrate the castle from the outside, using tools like grappling hooks and climbing gear to scale its walls or access its roof. Once on the roof, shinobi could use their skills in stealth and observation to gather intelligence on the castle's layout and defenses, as well as identify potential weaknesses or vulnerabilities.

Shinobi were also known to use diversionary tactics to distract the guards and create opportunities for infiltration. This might include setting fires or creating loud noises to draw attention away from their actual point of entry.

Overall, infiltrating a castle was a challenging and dangerous mission that required careful planning, specialized skills, and a willingness to take risks. However, shinobi were highly skilled and resourceful agents who were often successful in carrying out these kinds of covert operations.

ENTERING METHODS

The "Bansenshukai" contains several sections that describe how ninja could pick locks. One section, for example, discusses the use of a tool called a "kagi-nawa," which was a small hook attached to a length of cord or string.

To use the kagi-nawa, the ninja would insert the hook into the keyhole of a lock and then manipulate it to try and catch the tumblers inside. Once the tumblers were caught, the ninja could then use the cord or string to turn the lock and open the door.

Another section of the "Bansenshukai" describes a technique known as "tsurigane," which involved using a piece of wire or thin metal to create a new key for a lock. The ninja would carefully study the shape and design of the lock, and then use the wire to create a replica of the key that would fit into the lock and turn it.

STEALTH

The ninja were renowned for their stealth techniques, which allowed them to move silently and remain undetected while gathering information or carrying out missions.

DISGUISE

Hensojutsu, also known as disguise techniques, is a set of skills employed by ninja to change their appearance, clothing, and behavior to avoid detection and deceive their enemies. The techniques of hensojutsu include wearing disguises such as clothes of different professions or social status, makeup, and changing hairstyle or hair color. They may also use acting skills to play a role or mimic someone's behavior or mannerisms. The aim of hensojutsu is to blend in with the surroundings and appear as someone or something else, enabling the ninja to infiltrate, gather information, and execute their mission without being detected.

The shinobi, or ninja, were skilled in the art of disguise, and they would often use various disguises to infiltrate enemy territory or to gather information without being detected. Some common disguises used by the shinobi include:

1. Buddhist monks: Shinobi would often disguise themselves as Buddhist monks or other religious figures, as they were less likely to be suspected or questioned. They would dress in the attire of the monk and use religious symbols or artifacts to enhance their disguise.
2. Merchants: Shinobi would sometimes disguise themselves as merchants or traders, as this would allow them to move freely through towns and cities without arousing suspicion. They would carry goods or products that were typical of the area they were infiltrating to blend in with the local population.
3. Samurai: Shinobi would occasionally pose as samurai, the warrior class of feudal Japan. This would allow them to move through areas where samurai were expected, such as castles or other fortified areas.
4. Women: Shinobi would also use female disguises to infiltrate certain areas, as women were often underestimated and overlooked by their opponents. They would dress as geishas, female servants, or other women of the area they were infiltrating.
5. Peasants: Shinobi would sometimes disguise themselves as peasants or commoners, as this would allow them to move unnoticed through rural areas or small towns. They would dress in the clothing of the local peasants and adopt their mannerisms to blend in.

These are just a few examples of the many disguises used by the shinobi. They were highly skilled in the art of disguise and would often use a combination of disguises and other tactics to achieve their objectives.

IMPERSONATION

One of the ninja's special skills was the art of impersonation or disguise. It involves assuming a particular character or persona to gain access to restricted areas or to blend in with a particular group of people.

A range of techniques were developed to imitate the sounds of animals, such as birds and insects, as well as human sounds, such as coughing or sneezing. By doing so, a ninja could avoid detection and move about unnoticed.

Ninja would also mimic the mannerisms and behavior of different people, such as samurai or peasants, to blend in with different social classes.

These are essential skills for a ninja, as it enables them to infiltrate enemy territory and gather intelligence without being detected.

SPY TACTICS

The ninja employed a wide range of spying tactics to gather intelligence and carry out their covert operations. Some of the most common tactics included:

1. Infiltration: One of the key tactics employed by the ninja was infiltration, which involved disguising themselves as ordinary people and infiltrating the target location. They often used forged documents or other forms of identification to blend in and avoid suspicion.
2. Observation: Once inside the target location, the ninja would use their skills in observation to gather information about the layout, defenses, and key personnel. They might also use hidden cameras or other forms of surveillance to capture visual or audio information.
3. Disguise: Disguise was a key tactic used by the ninja to blend in with their surroundings and avoid detection. They might use makeup, clothing, or other props to change their appearance and fool their enemies.
4. Sabotage: Sabotage was another tactic used by the ninja to disrupt their enemies' operations and weaken their defenses. This might involve setting fires, cutting supply lines, or creating other forms of chaos.
5. Espionage: Espionage was a critical component of the ninja's operations, and involved gathering intelligence about their enemies' plans and activities. This might involve intercepting messages, stealing documents, or bribing informants.

CLIMBING

The ninja were skilled climbers and used a variety of techniques to scale walls, trees, and other structures. Some of the most common climbing methods used by the ninja included:

1. Handholds and footholds: The ninja would use handholds and footholds to climb up a wall or structure. These might be natural cracks and crevices in the wall or they could be created using tools such as spikes or hooks.
2. Rope climbing: The ninja were skilled at using ropes to climb up walls or trees. They might use a grappling hook to throw a rope over a wall, or they might tie the rope around their body and use their hands and feet to climb up.
3. Tree climbing: The ninja were also skilled at climbing trees, which allowed them to observe their surroundings from a high vantage point. They might use a rope to swing from branch to branch or use their hands and feet to climb up the trunk of the tree.
4. Wall running: The ninja were known for their ability to run up walls, which allowed them to scale structures quickly and efficiently. They might use their feet and legs to push off the wall and gain momentum, or they might use a combination of hand and foot holds to climb up.

WATER CROSSING

Crossing rivers and bodies of water was an important skill for the ninja, and they employed various techniques to do so. One common method was to tie a rope between two trees or other solid objects on opposite sides of the river, and then use the rope to traverse the water while holding on to it.

Another technique was to use a special kind of footwear called "mizugumo," which had allowed the ninja to swim faster and more efficiently. They could also use a small boat or raft, or even create makeshift flotation devices out of bamboo or other materials.

In some cases, the ninja would use diversion tactics to create a distraction and then cross the river or body of water undetected. For example, they might start a fire or make loud noises to draw attention away from their crossing point.

SILENT TRAVEL

The ninja had several silent walking methods, which were a crucial part of their stealth techniques.

A basic ninja walking technique involves walking quietly and slowly with the weight on the balls of the feet.

Another method involves crouching down low and moving forward in short, quick steps, like a baby bird (uzura) trying to walk for the first time.

There is also a way of using the feet to feel the ground for any uneven surfaces or obstacles, allowing the ninja to move more silently and safely.

ESCAPE

The ninja were highly skilled at escape and evasion, and employed a variety of techniques to evade capture or escape from dangerous situations. Some of the most common escape methods used by the ninja included:

1. Disguise: The ninja would often use disguises to blend in with their surroundings and avoid detection. They might change their clothing, hairstyle, or makeup to look like someone else, or they might use props such as hats or walking sticks to alter their appearance.
2. Concealment: The ninja were masters of concealment, and could hide in plain sight by blending into their surroundings or using camouflage techniques. They might hide behind objects, crawl along the ground, or use natural cover such as trees or bushes to stay hidden.
3. Deception: The ninja were skilled at deception, and might use diversionary tactics to distract their pursuers or throw them off their trail. They might create false trails, set decoys, or use other tricks to confuse their enemies.

4. Speed and agility: The ninja were also known for their speed and agility, and could use their acrobatic skills to evade pursuit. They might run, jump, or climb over obstacles, or use parkour-style techniques to move quickly and efficiently through their environment.
5. Weapons and tools: The ninja were experts in the use of weapons and tools, and might use throwing stars, smoke bombs, or other tools to distract or incapacitate their enemies. They might also use ropes or grappling hooks to escape from high places or climb over walls.

Overall, the ninja were highly skilled at escape and evasion, and used a range of techniques to stay one step ahead of their enemies. Their ability to blend in with their surroundings, move quickly and efficiently, and use deception and diversionary tactics made them some of the most effective escape artists in history.

DIET

The diet of the ninja was largely based on what was available in their region and depended on their mission and circumstances. However, the ninja were known for being highly skilled in gathering food from the wild and were able to survive on very little.

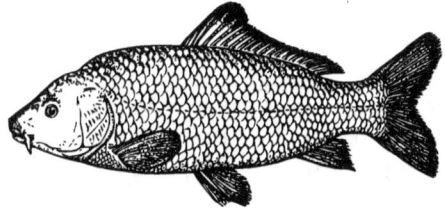

Some of the common foods that the ninja ate included:

- Rice: Rice was a staple food in Japan and was commonly eaten by the ninja.
- Fish: The ninja often lived near water sources and were skilled at catching fish to supplement their diet.
- Vegetables: The ninja would gather wild vegetables such as mushrooms, wild onions, and other edible plants.
- Meat: The ninja were also skilled hunters and would catch small game such as rabbits or birds to supplement their diet.
- Nuts and seeds: The ninja would gather nuts and seeds from the wild, such as acorns, chestnuts, and sesame seeds, which provided essential nutrients.

In addition to these foods, the ninja were also known for carrying small, portable food items with them on missions, such as dried meat, rice cakes, and pickled vegetables. These items could be eaten quickly and provided the ninja with the energy they needed to complete their missions.

KUJI KIRI

Kuji-kiri is a practice that involves the use of hand gestures, or mudras, to channel energy and achieve various effects. It is often associated with Japanese esoteric Buddhism and ninja traditions.

The practice of kuji-kiri involves tracing a series of hand gestures while reciting a mantra or meditation. There are various hand gestures associated with kuji-kiri, each of which is said to correspond with a specific energy or intention.

In some ninja traditions, kuji-kiri was used as a form of spiritual and physical training, as well as a method of focus and concentration during combat. It was believed that by performing kuji-kiri, a ninja could enhance their abilities, including their agility, strength, and senses, as well as protect themselves from harm.

Today, kuji-kiri is still practiced by some martial artists and spiritual practitioners in Japan and other parts of the world. However, its exact origins and historical significance remain a subject of debate and speculation among scholars and practitioners.

フウ
THE
WIND SCROLL
SECTION THREE

EQUIPMENT

Tools, weapons & clothing

I n the world of the ninja, the right clothing, tools, and
weapons could mean the difference between life and
death. The ninja's arsenal was as varied as it was deadly,
from throwing stars to swords, from grappling hooks to smoke
bombs. And the clothing they wore was not just for protection
against the elements, but also served to help them blend into
their surroundings and move with agility and stealth.

In this chapter, we will explore ninja apparel, delve into the
various tools and weapons that the ninja used, examine their
purposes and how they were used in the field.

By understanding the clothing, tools, and weapons of the ninja,
we can gain a deeper appreciation for their methods and their
effectiveness.

Let's enter the world of the ninja and explore the equipment
that made them one of the most feared and respected warrior
groups in history.

CLOTHING

The shinobi, or ninja, did not have a specific uniform or clothing that was distinct from the general population of feudal Japan. This was because the shinobi needed to blend in with their surroundings and not draw attention to themselves. However, there were certain clothing items that were commonly used by shinobi to aid in their missions. These included:

1. Tabi: Tabi are traditional Japanese socks that have a split toe design, which allows the wearer to wear them with sandals or other footwear. The shinobi often wore tabi to aid in their stealth movements, as the split toe design allowed them to move more silently and with greater agility.
2. Hachimaki: The hachimaki is a traditional Japanese headband that was sometimes worn by the shinobi. The hachimaki could be used to keep sweat out of the eyes or to cover the face and disguise the wearer's identity.

These are just a few examples of the clothing and equipment that were commonly used by the shinobi. The shinobi were highly skilled in adapting their clothing and equipment to suit the mission at hand, and they were known for their ability to improvise and use whatever tools were available to them.

Zukin & Fukumen (Hood and mask)

Tekoh (sleeves / gloves)

Uwagi (jacket)

Hakama (trousers)

Kyahan (leg wraps)

THE OUTFIT

Tabi (split toe footwear)

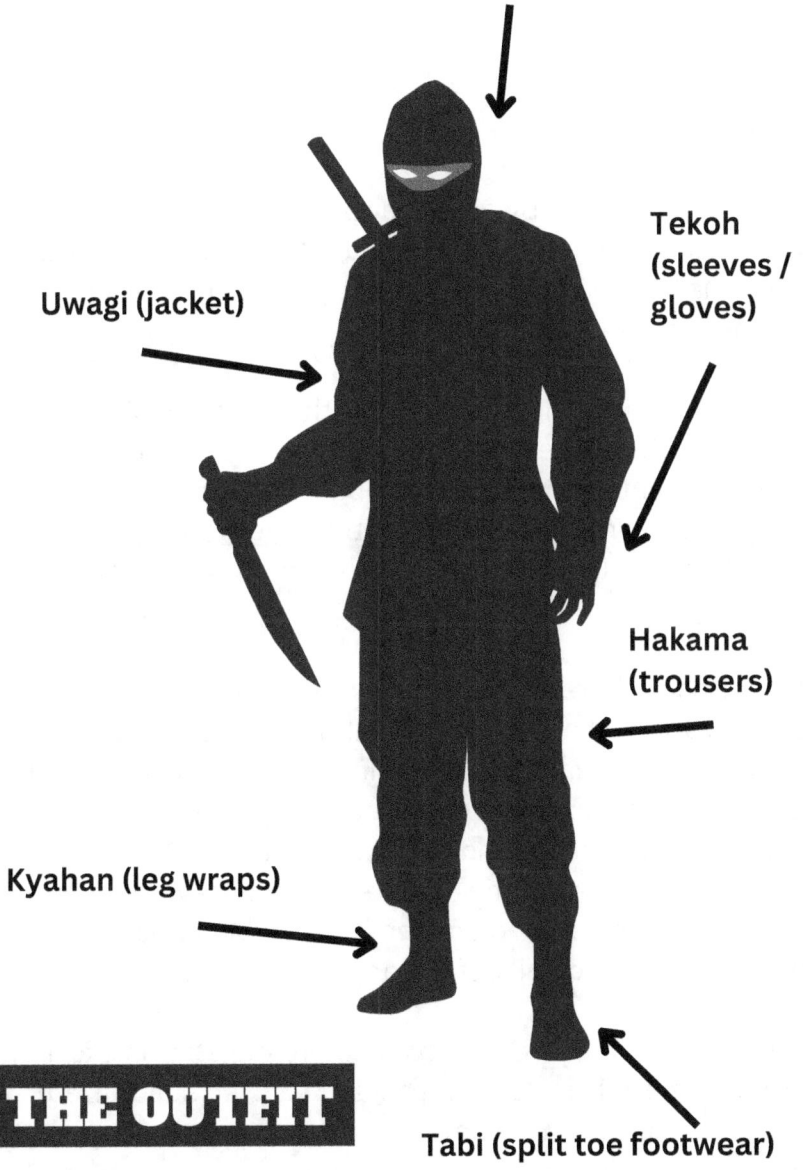

ARMOUR

While the use of armor by ninja is a topic of some debate among historians and martial arts practitioners, it is generally believed that ninja did not wear traditional samurai armor during their missions.

This is because the weight and bulk of the armor would have made it difficult for the ninja to move quickly and quietly, which was essential to their stealth-based tactics. Instead, ninja typically wore lightweight, unobtrusive clothing that allowed them to blend in with their surroundings and move more freely.

That being said, there are some accounts of ninja using specialized armor that was specifically designed for their unique needs. For example, some ninja are said to have worn armor made from chainmail or leather, which offered some protection against blows and cuts while still allowing for flexibility and mobility. Other ninja are said to have used armor made from woven bamboo or even paper, which was lightweight but could still deflect arrows or shuriken.

Overall, while armor was not a common feature of ninja attire, there were certainly instances where ninja used specialized armor as part of their missions.

TOOLS ASSOCIATED WITH THE NINJA

The shinobi, or ninja, were skilled at using a wide variety of tools to aid in their missions. These tools included both weapons and everyday objects that could be used in creative and unexpected ways. Here are some examples of tools commonly associated with the shinobi:

1. Shuriken: Used by the shinobi for both attacking and distracting their enemies. Shuriken were often designed with sharp edges or points that could cause serious injury or distraction.
2. Smoke bombs: The shinobi sometimes used smoke bombs to create a diversion or to obscure their movements from their enemies. Smoke bombs could be made using a variety of materials, such as gunpowder or natural ingredients like pepper.
3. Grappling hook: The grappling hook is a tool that the shinobi used to climb walls or trees quickly and silently. The hook could be attached to a rope or chain and thrown up to the top of a wall or tree to create a secure anchor for climbing.
4. Makibishi: Makibishi are small metal spikes that were scattered on the ground to slow down pursuers or to injure horses. The shinobi would carry makibishi with them and drop them behind them as they fled, making it difficult for their pursuers to catch up.
5. Kama: The kama is a sickle-like weapon that was used by the shinobi for both combat and farming. The sharp blade of the kama could be used to cut through vegetation, as well as to disarm or injure an opponent.

6 ESSENTIAL NINJA TOOLS

AMIGASA

A Japanese straw hat. Good for hiding the face or stowing hidden weapons.

KAGINAWA

Rope and hook. Used for climbing and a multitude of other purposes.

SEKIHITSU

Writing set. Stone pencil, brush & ink for communication.

KUSURI

First aid kit kept in an inro box.

UCHI-TAKE

Bamboo tube for embers. Could be used to warm the body.

TENUGUI

Multi-purpose towel. 3 shaku in length. Use to cover face & filter water.

NINJA SWORDS

There is no specific sword that is associated exclusively with ninjas. However, the ninja did use a variety of weapons, including swords, that were similar to those used by samurai warriors of the time.

The most common sword used by the ninja was the katana, which was a long, curved sword that was designed for cutting. The ninja also used shorter swords, such as the wakizashi, which could be used for close-quarters combat.

One weapon that is often associated with the ninja is the ninjato, which is sometimes referred to as the "ninja sword." However, there is little historical evidence to suggest that this sword was actually used by the ninja. The ninjato is a straight sword with a shorter blade than the katana and was allegedly designed for use in tight spaces and for quick, silent strikes. However, many historians believe that the ninjato is a fictional weapon that was popularized in movies and literature rather than being based on historical fact.

In summary, while there is no specific sword that is associated exclusively with ninjas, the ninja did use a variety of swords and other weapons that were similar to those used by samurai warriors of the time.

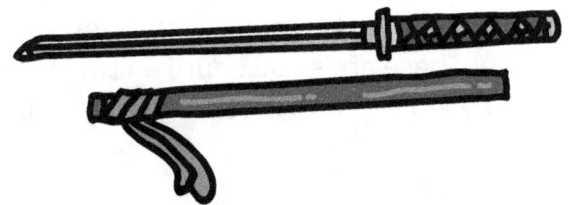

SHURIKEN

A shuriken, also known as a "ninja star," is a small, handheld weapon that was used in feudal Japan by warriors, including the ninja. It is typically made of metal and has a star-like shape, with sharpened edges that allow it to be thrown or used in close combat. Shuriken were originally designed as a concealed weapon, and some were specifically created to resemble everyday objects such as hairpins or coins. They were primarily used for distraction or to disable an opponent rather than for killing, although some shuriken were designed to be lethal.

Shuriken, which means "sword hidden in the hand," had various designs.

1. Bo shuriken: These are long, narrow, and pointed shuriken that were originally used as throwing darts.
2. Hira shuriken: These are flat, star-shaped shuriken with four to eight points. They were primarily used as throwing weapons, but could also be used for slashing attacks.
3. Tanto shuriken: These are small shuriken that were shaped like knives and used for both throwing and stabbing.

The senban shuriken is a type of shuriken that has four equally sized points and is typically used for throwing. Here is a basic guide on how to throw a senban shuriken:

1. Hold the shuriken between your thumb and index finger with the tips of the points facing forward.
2. Place your middle finger on the flat part of the shuriken with your ring and pinky fingers supporting it from below.
3. Bring your arm back and then swing it forward towards your target, releasing the shuriken as you do so.
4. Aim for the target, taking into account the distance and trajectory needed to hit it accurately.
5. Follow through with your throw, extending your arm fully in the direction of your target.

It's important to note that throwing shuriken requires a lot of practice and should only be done in a safe environment with proper supervision. It's also important to follow all laws and regulations regarding the possession and use of shuriken in your area.

MORE TOOLS OF THE NINJA

KAMA

A sickle or scythe. Used for cutting but can be attached to a cord and used for climbing.

KUNAI

A digger tool. But can be used as a weapon or a climbing aid.

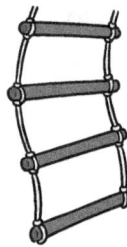

HASHIGO

Various types of ladders. Some were constructed from rope and bamboo.

MAKIBISHI

Caltrops to slow down the persuing enemy. Can be natural water chestnuts or made of iron.

NATA

A useful tool for cutting bamboo. A lot like a machete.

フウ
THE
EARTH SCROLL
SECTION FOUR

NINJA BOOM

The "ninja boom" refers to a period of increased popularity and interest in ninja culture and mythology that occurred in Japan and around the world during the 1980s and 1990s. This trend was sparked by a combination of factors, including the success of several popular ninja-themed movies and TV shows, as well as the publication of numerous books and magazines on the topic.

One of the key drivers of the ninja boom was the success of the "Ninja" series of films, which were produced by the Japanese studio Toei in the 1960s and 1970s. These movies featured colorful, acrobatic depictions of ninja fighting and espionage, and were hugely popular with Japanese audiences. The films were later dubbed into English and released in the West, where they became cult favorites and helped to fuel interest in ninja culture.

Another factor that contributed to the ninja boom was the availability of information about the history and techniques of ninjutsu. During this period, a number of books and magazines on the subject were published in Japan, which helped to create a new generation of fans and practitioners of the art.

Additionally, a number of martial arts schools began to incorporate elements of ninjutsu into their training programs, further boosting interest in the art.

The ninja boom also had a significant impact on popular culture outside of Japan. In the United States and Europe, numerous ninja-themed movies, TV shows, and comic books were produced during the 1980s and 1990s, helping to establish the ninja as an iconic figure in popular culture. Today, the legacy of the ninja boom can still be seen in the continued popularity of ninja-themed media and the enduring fascination with ninja culture and mythology.

NINJUTSU TODAY

Modern ninjutsu is a term used to describe various martial arts and self-defense systems that claim to be based on traditional ninjutsu techniques and principles. These practices are typically taught in martial arts schools and training centers around the world.

Modern ninjutsu schools often incorporate a variety of techniques, including striking, grappling, joint locks, throws, and weapons training. Some schools also teach stealth and espionage techniques, as well as principles of strategy and tactics.

One of the key features of modern ninjutsu is its emphasis on practical self-defense applications.

Many schools focus on teaching techniques that can be used in real-world self-defense situations, rather than just for sport or competition. This often includes training in multiple attackers, weapons attacks, and other scenarios that may occur in a self-defense situation.

In addition to physical training, modern ninjutsu schools often incorporate mental and spiritual development into their practice. This may include meditation, breathing exercises, and other practices aimed at developing focus, discipline, and inner strength.

NATORI RYU

Natori-Ryu is a traditional Japanese martial arts school that originated in the Edo period (1603-1868) and focuses on the techniques and strategies of the ninja. It was founded by Natori Masazumi, who was a direct descendant of Natori Shoto, a legendary ninja who served the Tokugawa shogunate.

The Natori-Ryu curriculum includes training in a variety of skills, such as stealth and infiltration techniques, intelligence gathering, and the use of various tools.

The system has been resurrected by author & historian Antony Cummins with the support of the Natori family & the Eunji Temple.

KATORI SHINTO RYU

Katori Shinto Ryu is a traditional Japanese martial art that dates back to the 14th century. While it is not primarily focused on ninjutsu, the school includes techniques and strategies for dealing with ninja attacks and infiltration.

According to the Katori Shinto Ryu tradition, the founder of the school, Iizasa Choisai Ienao, was a skilled warrior who trained in both the samurai and ninja arts. He is said to have created the school after a dream in which he received teachings from a divine spirit.

The Katori Shinto Ryu curriculum includes a variety of weapons, including the sword, spear, and naginata, as well as grappling techniques and unarmed combat. Some of the techniques in the school are designed specifically to counter the tactics of ninja, such as techniques for detecting hidden weapons and spotting hidden attackers.

The school also emphasizes strategy and tactics, including methods for analyzing an enemy's strengths and weaknesses and adapting to changing circumstances on the battlefield.

Practice today is led by Ōtake Nobutoshi Shihan. The tradition was passed down from his father Ōtake Risuke Shihan (1926 -2021).

The headquarters of the Shinbukan Dōjō is situated in the countryside near Narita City, Chiba Prefecture, Japan.

Tenshinshō-den Katori Shintō-ryū is preserved and transmitted both domestically and internationally.

TOGAKURE RYU

Togakure Ryu is a martial arts school that is often associated with the ninja. The origins of the Togakure Ryu can be traced back to the 12th century, when the founder of the school, Daisuke Nishina, is said to have fled to the mountains to avoid persecution during a time of political upheaval. While living in the mountains, Nishina is said to have learned martial arts from a group of tengu, supernatural beings from Japanese folklore.

Over time, the techniques and philosophy of the Togakure Ryu were refined and passed down through a lineage of masters. One of the most famous of these masters was Toda Shinryuken, who is credited with codifying the teachings of the Togakure Ryu and passing them on to his student, Toshitsugu Takamatsu.

Takamatsu, in turn, taught the techniques of the Togakure Ryu to his own students, including Masaaki Hatsumi, who is perhaps the most well-known modern exponent of the art. Hatsumi founded the Bujinkan organization, which teaches the techniques of several traditional Japanese martial arts schools, including the Togakure Ryu.

It is worth noting that the historical accuracy of the Togakure Ryu's origins and lineage has been called into question by some scholars and martial arts historians. Nevertheless, the school and its techniques remain an important part of the modern popular image of the ninja.

KAWAKAMI

Jinichi Kawakami is a Japanese martial artist and historian who is widely recognized as the last living master of authentic ninjutsu. He was born in 1949 in Iga, Japan, which was historically known as one of the centers of ninja activity. Kawakami began studying martial arts at a young age, and eventually became interested in the history and techniques of ninjutsu.

In addition to his martial arts training, Kawakami also conducted extensive research into the history and culture of the ninja.

Kawakami is known for his efforts to preserve and promote the authentic traditions of ninjutsu, and has been recognized by the Japanese government for his contributions to cultural preservation. Despite his advanced age, he continues to teach and train others in the art of ninjutsu, and remains an important figure in the world of martial arts and historical research.

POP CULTURE

Ninja have had a significant impact on popular culture, both in Japan and around the world. They have become iconic figures in popular culture, often portrayed as skilled and stealthy assassins who are masters of various weapons and martial arts. Some of the ways in which ninja have influenced popular culture include:

1. Media: Ninja have been featured in a wide variety of media, including movies, TV shows, anime, manga, video games, and more. Popular examples include the "Naruto" manga and anime series, the "Shinobi" video game series, and the "Teenage Mutant Ninja Turtles" franchise.
2. Fashion: Ninja clothing and accessories, such as black masks and throwing stars, have become popular fashion items in Japan and around the world.
3. Sports: Modern-day sports such as parkour and free running have been influenced by the movements and techniques of the ninja.
4. Tourism: Many cities and towns in Japan with historical ties to ninja have become popular tourist destinations, offering visitors the chance to experience ninja-themed attractions and activities.

The legacy of ninjutsu continues to live on today. While some aspects of traditional ninjutsu may have been lost over time, modern practitioners are working to keep the art alive by studying historical texts, training in the physical skills and techniques, and adapting them to modern contexts.

FURTHER RESEARCH

There are several researchers and scholars who are actively studying and researching ninjutsu today. Some of the leading figures in the field include:

1. Antony Cummins: Cummins is a historian, author, and researcher who specializes in the study of ninjutsu and Japanese martial arts. He has written several books on the subject, including "True Path of the Ninja" and "The Secret Traditions of the Shinobi."
2. Dr. Kacem Zoughari: Dr. Zoughari is a French scholar and researcher who specializes in the study of Japanese martial arts and culture. He has written several books on the subject, including "The Ninja: Myth, Reality, and Legacy."
3. Dr. Stephen Turnbull: Dr. Turnbull is a British historian and author who has written extensively on Japanese history and culture. He has written several books on the ninja, including "Ninja: Unmasking the Myth" and "Ninja: The True Story of Japan's Secret Warrior Cult."
4. Dr. Mikio Yahara: Dr. Yahara is a Japanese martial artist and researcher who has written several books on the history and techniques of ninjutsu. He is also the founder of the Yahara Martial Arts Academy in Japan.
5. Dr. Masaaki Hatsumi: Dr. Hatsumi is a Japanese martial artist and researcher who is considered one of the foremost experts on ninjutsu. He is the founder of the Bujinkan Dojo, which teaches a variety of martial arts and ninjutsu techniques.

忍 INDEX

Art of War   30
Climbing   42
Clothing   51
Diet   45
Disguise   37
Entering methods   36
Escape   44
Hattori Hanzo   21
Infiltration   34
Kama   59
Katori Shinto Ryu   64
Kuji Kiri   47
Natori Ryu   64
Ninja   10
Samurai   21
Shuriken   57
Stealth   37
Sword   56
Togakure Ryu   66
Tools   54
Water crossing   43

www.ingramcontent.com/pod-product-compliance
Lightning Source LLC
Chambersburg PA
CBHW060644290526
45793CB00001B/383